The Ultimate Outdoor Gas Griddle Cookbook

Delicious Recipes for Grilling, Searing, and More

Thaddeus Davis

Copyright © 2023 - All rights reserved.

The content contained within this book may not be reproduced, duplicated, or transmitted without direct written permission from the author or the publisher.

Under no circumstances will any blame or legal responsibility be held against the publisher, or author, for any damages, reparation, or monetary loss due to the information contained within this book. Either directly or indirectly.

Legal Notice: This book is copyright protected. This book is only for personal use. You cannot amend, distribute, sell, use, quote, or paraphrase any part, or the content within this book, without the consent of the author or publisher.

Disclaimer Notice: Please note the information contained within this document is for educational and entertainment purposes only. All effort has been executed to present accurate, up-to-date, and reliable, complete information. No warranties of any kind are declared or implied. Readers acknowledge that the author is not engaging in the rendering of legal, financial, medical, or professional advice. The content within this book has been derived from various sources. Please consult a licensed professional before attempting any techniques outlined in this book.

By reading this document, the reader agrees that under no circumstances is the author responsible for any losses, direct or indirect, which are incurred as a result of the use of the information contained within this document, including, but not limited to, — errors, omissions, or inaccuracies.

Table of Contents

Gas Griddle Vs Wooden Pellet Grill _____ 5
Gas Griddle Cooking Table _____ 7
Maintenance _____ 9
Conversion Tables _____ 10
Breakfast Recipes _____ 12
    Perfect Scrambled Eggs _____ 13
    Buttermilk Pancakes _____ 14
    Strawberry, Banana, and Hazelnut-Chocolate Crepes _____ 16
    Steak and Mushroom Crepes _____ 18
    Griddled Cheese Breakfast Burrito _____ 20
    Chorizo Breakfast Tacos _____ 22
Burger's Recipes _____ 24
    Juicy Texas Burgers _____ 25
    Porky Burger _____ 27
    Texas Burger with Beer Cheese Sauce _____ 29
    Homemade Veggie Burger _____ 31
    St. Louis Gerber Pork Burger _____ 33
    White Cheddar Turkey Smash Burger with Apple Slaw _____ 35
Vegetables & Side dishes _____ 37
    Bacon and Corn Griddle Cakes _____ 38
    Hibachi Vegetables _____ 40
    Griddle Vegetable Quesadillas _____ 42
    Maple Bacon Brussels Sprouts _____ 44
    Crispy Fried Green Tomatoes _____ 45
    Griddled Vegetables with Melting Aubergines _____ 47
Beef Recipes _____ 49
    Flash-Marinated Skirt Steak _____ 50
    Homemade Meatballs _____ 52
    Copycat Texas Roadhouse Steak _____ 54

Griddle Steak Bites	56
Grilled Beef Tenderloin with Herb-Garlic-Pepper Coating	58
Sirloin Wrapped Jalapeño Poppers	60
Pork Recipes	**62**
Perfect Pork Chops	63
Smoky Grilled Pork Chops	64
Marinated Pork Skewers	66
Griddled Pork And Peaches	68
Griddle Pork Fried Rice	70
Simple Smoked Pulled Pork Butt	72
Chicken Recipes	**74**
Seared Chicken Breasts	75
Chicken Teriyaki	76
Chicken Fried Rice	78
Perfect Chicken Wings	80
Chicken Lo Mein	81
Chicken With Mushroom Gravy	83
Poultry Recipes	**85**
Herb Roasted Turkey	86
Marinated Smoked Turkey Breast	88
Brined Grilled Turkey With Maple Bourbon Glaze	90
Lamb Recipes	**92**
Griddled Lamb With Spiced New Potatoes	93
Garlic Butter Lamb Chops	95
Garlic & Rosemary Grilled Lamb Chops	96
Dessert Recipes	**97**
Griddle Monkey Bread With Biscuits	98
Grilled Smore's Pizza	100
Griddle Cinnamon Rolls	101
Extra Lofty Griddle Cakes	103
Chocolate Griddle Cakes	105
Rum-Glazed Griddled Pineapple	107

Gas Griddle Vs Wooden Pellet Grill

One significant difference between the gas griddle and the wood pellet grill is the fuel source. A gas griddle is fueled by natural gas or propane, whereas a wood pellet grill uses wood pellets as fuel, which affects the outcome of the dishes. For example, there is a considerable difference in temperature and heat distribution. Gas griddles generally heat up more quickly and provide more even heat distribution, making it easier to cook foods uniformly and to the desired degree of doneness. Wood pellet grills, on the other hand, take more time to heat up and may have hotter and cooler spots, making it harder to achieve consistent results.

In terms of maintenance and upkeep, gas griddles are generally more manageable to maintain than wood pellet grills because of the ash produced by burning wood pellets. Hence, wood pellet grills may require frequent cleaning, and the pellets need to be refilled.

Regarding taste, the wood chips produce a smoky flavor that enhances the quality of many dishes, but it may not be suitable for all recipes. Some people do not like the smokiness, making the quality of the outcome subjective. However, with wood pellet grills, you cannot avoid the grill's flavor on your food.

Gas griddles can be compared to charcoal grills, as both give off a distinct flavor that may or may not suit the dish and is an acquired taste. Charcoal grills are easier to transport and use at picnics, but the process of getting the charcoal briquettes lit and evenly distributing the cinders is an art that requires experience. Moreover, relying on coal for heat makes it challenging to control the temperature and heat distribution.

Operating and using these grills can be more time-consuming and require more maintenance than gas griddles. They usually take longer to heat up and may have hotter and cooler spots, making it more challenging to achieve consistent cooking results. Additionally, they produce ash, which requires regular cleaning and maintenance.

Gas Griddle Cooking Table

Now that we're all set for cooking, here's a quick reference table that shows the recommended temperature and time for cooking certain foods. Please keep in mind that these are general guidelines, and actual cooking times may vary based on factors such as the size and thickness of the meat, the recipe, and your desired level of doneness. For best results, I also recommend using a meat thermometer to ensure that the meat has reached the desired internal temperature.

Meat Type	Recommended Cooking Temperature	Recommended Cooking Time
Burgers (beef, turkey, veggie)	375-400°F	4-6 minutes per side
Steaks (beef, pork, lamb)	400-450°F	4-6 minutes per side
Pork chops	400-450°F	6-8 minutes per side
Chicken	375-400°F	6-8 minutes per side
Turkey	375-400°F	6-8 minutes per side
Duck	400-450°F	4-6 minutes per side
Rabbit	375-400°F	6-8 minutes per side
Shrimp	375-400°F	2-3 minutes per side
Salmon	375-400°F	4-6 minutes per side

Vegetables (zucchini, bell peppers, onions)	375-400°F	4-6 minutes per side
Pulled pork	275-300°F	6-8 hours
Slow cooked dark meat	275-300°F	6-8 hours
Elk	400-450°F	4-6 minutes per side
Boar	400-450°F	4-6 minutes per side

Maintenance

Proper maintenance is essential to ensure that your gas griddle stays in good working condition and continues to perform at its best. Here are some tips for maintaining your gas griddle:

1. **Clean the griddle surface after each use:** Wipe down the griddle surface with a damp cloth or sponge to remove any excess food or grease. This will help to prevent flare-ups and ensure that your griddle stays in good condition.
2. **Use a griddle scraper:** A griddle scraper is a tool specifically designed to remove stuckon food and debris from the griddle surface. It is an effective and safe way to keep your griddle clean without damaging the surface.
3. **Remove excess grease:** After each use, it is important to remove excess grease from the griddle surface and grease tray. This can be done using a griddle scraper, a sponge, or a paper towel.
4. **Store your griddle properly:** When not in use, make sure to cover your gas griddle with a protective cover to keep it clean and protected from the elements.
5. **Check for gas leaks:** Regularly check the gas hose and regulator for any signs of wear or damage. If you notice any leaks, make sure to fix them immediately.
6. **Replace worn or damaged parts:** If any parts of your gas griddle are worn or damaged, make sure to replace them as soon as possible to ensure that your griddle stays in good working condition.

By following these maintenance tips, you can help to extend the life of your gas griddle and ensure that it continues to perform at its best.

Conversion Tables

We are almost done with this section and before we get on to the recipes, here are a few tables with the conversion of various units of measurements that may come in handy:

Temperature conversions:

Fahrenheit	Celsius
250°F	121.1°C
275°F	135.0°C
300°F	148.9°C
325°F	162.8°C
350°F	176.7°C
375°F	190.6°C
400°F	204.4°C
425°F	218.3°C
450°F	232.2°C

Weight conversions:

Pounds	Kilograms
1 lb	0.45 kg
2 lbs	0.91 kg
3 lbs	1.36 kg
4 lbs	1.81 kg
5 lbs	2.27 kg

Volume conversions:

Fluid ounces	Milliliters
1 fl oz	29.57 ml
2 fl oz	59.15 ml
3 fl oz	88.72 ml
4 fl oz	118.29 ml
5 fl oz	147.87 ml

Breakfast Recipes

Perfect Scrambled Eggs

Scrambled eggs are a classic breakfast dish that can be easily prepared on a gas griddle. They are a quick and easy meal that can be enjoyed any time of day.

Serving size: 1-2 people | Preparation time: 10 minutes

Griddling time: 5-7 minutes | Griddle temperature: 375-400°F.

Prepare Ingredients

- 2-3 large eggs
- 1 tablespoon butter or oil
- Salt and pepper, to taste

Start the Griddle

1. Crack the eggs into a small bowl and beat them lightly with a fork.
2. Place the butter or oil on the griddle and allow it to melt.
3. Pour the beaten eggs onto the griddle and use a spatula to scrape the bottom of the griddle as the eggs cook.
4. Once the eggs start to set, use the spatula to gently fold them over and scramble them until they are fully cooked.
5. Season the eggs with salt and pepper, to taste.
6. Serve the scrambled eggs hot, with your choice of accompaniments such as toast, bacon, or fruit.

Nutritional Value (Per Serving)

- Calories: 150
- Protein: 12 g
- Fat: 11 g
- Carbs: 1 g
- Fiber: 0 g
- Sugars: 1 g

Buttermilk Pancakes

Soft and fluffy on the inside, with a golden brown crust on the outside, these pancakes are sure to satisfy your cravings.

Serving size: 10 medium-sized pancakes | Preparation time: 15 minutes to prepare | Griddling time: 10-15 minutes to cook. | Griddle temperature: 375-400°F.

Prepare Ingredients

- 1 cup all-purpose flour
- 1 teaspoon baking powder
- 1/2 teaspoon baking soda
- 1/2 teaspoon salt
- 1 cup buttermilk
- 1 large egg
- 2 tablespoons butter, melted
- 1 teaspoon vanilla extract
- Cooking spray or butter, for greasing the griddle

Start the Griddle

1. Griddling process:
2. In a medium mixing bowl, whisk together the flour, baking powder, baking soda, and salt.
3. In a separate mixing bowl, whisk together the buttermilk, egg, melted butter, and vanilla extract.
4. Add the wet ingredients to the dry ingredients and stir until just combined. The batter should be slightly lumpy.
5. Heat the griddle over medium heat and lightly grease it with cooking spray or butter.
6. Pour the batter onto the griddle in 1/4 cup increments, using a spoon or ladle to spread it into circles.
7. Cook the pancakes for 2-3 minutes, or until bubbles start to form on the surface.
8. Flip the pancakes and cook for an additional 1-2 minutes, or

until golden brown on the second side.
9. Remove the pancakes from the griddle and place them on a plate. Repeat the process with the remaining batter, lightly greasing the griddle as needed.
10. Serve the pancakes hot, with your choice of toppings such as syrup, butter, fruit, or whipped cream.

Nutritional Value (Per Serving)

- Calories: 150
- Protein: 4 g
- Fat: 6 g
- Carbs: 22 g
- Fiber: 1 g

Strawberry, Banana, and Hazelnut-Chocolate Crepes

This classic French dish is filled with fresh strawberries, bananas, and a rich and creamy hazelnut-chocolate spread and makes a great breakfast.

Serving size: 8 crepes | Preparation time: 20 minutes

Griddling time: 10-15 minutes | Griddle temperature: 375-400°F

Prepare Ingredients

- 1 cup all-purpose flour
- 1 cup milk
- 1 large egg
- 2 tablespoons sugar
- 1 teaspoon vanilla extract
- 1/4 teaspoon salt
- 1 cup fresh strawberries, sliced
- 1 medium banana, sliced
- 1/2 cup hazelnut-chocolate spread
- Cooking spray or butter, for greasing the griddle

Start the Griddle

1. In a medium mixing bowl, whisk together the flour, milk, egg, sugar, vanilla extract, and salt.
2. Heat the griddle over medium heat and lightly grease it with cooking spray or butter.
3. Pour about 1/4 cup of the crepe batter onto the griddle, using a spoon or ladle to spread it into a thin, even circle.
4. Cook the crepe for 1-2 minutes, or until the edges start to turn golden brown.
5. Flip the crepe and cook for an additional 30 seconds, or until cooked through.
6. Remove the crepe from the griddle and place it on a plate. Repeat the process with the remaining batter, lightly greasing

the griddle as needed.
7. Once all the crepes are cooked, fill each crepe with a few slices of strawberry, banana, and a spoonful of hazelnut-chocolate spread.
8. Roll the crepes up and serve them hot.

Nutritional Value (Per Serving)

- Calories: 250
- Protein: 6 g
- Fat: 9 g
- Carbs: 41 g
- Fiber: 2 g
- Sugars: 21 g

Steak and Mushroom Crepes

Though crepes are mostly associated with sweets, this dish, with a savory flavor showcases another dimension that can be added to this French delicacy.

Serving size: 8 crepes | Preparation time: 30 minutes

Griddling time: 10-15 minutes | Griddle temperature: 375-400°F.

Prepare Ingredients

- 1 cup all-purpose flour
- 1 cup milk
- 1 large egg
- 1/4 teaspoon salt
- 1/2 pound thin-sliced steak, cut into strips
- 1 cup mushrooms, sliced
- 1 tablespoon butter or oil
- 1/4 cup shredded cheese (optional)
- Cooking spray or butter, for greasing the griddle

Start the Griddle

1. In a medium mixing bowl, whisk together the flour, milk, egg, and salt.
2. Heat the griddle over medium heat and lightly grease it with cooking spray or butter.
3. Pour about 1/4 cup of the crepe batter onto the griddle, using a spoon or ladle to spread it into a thin, even circle.
4. Cook the crepe for 1-2 minutes, or until the edges start to turn golden brown.
5. Flip the crepe and cook for an additional 30 seconds, or until cooked through.
6. Remove the crepe from the griddle and place it on a plate. Repeat the process with the remaining batter, lightly greasing the griddle as needed.
7. While the crepes are cooking, heat the butter or oil in a pan

over medium heat. Add the steak and mushrooms and sauté until the steak is cooked to your desired level of doneness and the mushrooms are tender.
8. Once all the crepes are cooked, fill each crepe with a few slices of steak and mushrooms. Sprinkle with cheese, if using.
9. Roll the crepes up and serve them hot

Nutritional Value (Per Serving)

- Calories: 250
- Protein: 20 g
- Fat: 9 g
- Carbs: 21 g
- Fiber: 2 g
- Sugars: 4 g

Griddled Cheese Breakfast Burrito

Filled with fluffy scrambled eggs, melted cheese, and a variety of toppings, this griddled cheese burrito is sure to hit the spot.

Serving size: 1 burrito | Preparation time: 10 minutes

Griddling time: 5-10 minutes | Griddle temperature: 375-400°F.

Prepare Ingredients

- 1 large flour tortilla
- 2 large eggs
- 1/4 cup shredded cheese
- 2 tablespoons diced cooked bacon, sausage, or ham (optional)
- 2 tablespoons diced bell pepper, onion, or tomato (optional)
- Cooking spray or butter, for greasing the griddle

Start the Griddle

1. Heat the griddle over medium heat and lightly grease it with cooking spray or butter.
2. In a small mixing bowl, beat the eggs until well scrambled.
3. Place the tortilla on the griddle and sprinkle the cheese over one-half of the tortilla.
4. Pour the eggs over the cheese and add the optional toppings, if using.
5. Fold the tortilla in half over the filling and press gently to seal.
6. Cook the burrito for 2-3 minutes, or until the bottom is golden brown and the cheese is melted.
7. Flip the burrito and cook for an additional 1-2 minutes, or until the second side is golden brown.
8. Remove the burrito from the griddle and cut it in half. Serve hot.

Nutritional Value (Per Serving)

- Calories: 350
- Protein: 20 g

- Fat: 20 g
- Carbs: 26 g
- Fiber: 2 g
- Sugars: 4 g

Chorizo Breakfast Tacos

If you love Mexican food and breakfast, these tacos filled with spicy chorizo sausage, fluffy scrambled eggs, and a variety of toppings are sure to satisfy your love.

Serving size: 4 tacos | Preparation time: 15 minutes

Griddling time: 5-10 minutes to cook

Griddle temperature: 375-400°F

Prepare Ingredients

- 4 small corn tortillas
- 1/2 cup diced chorizo sausage
- 2 large eggs
- 1/4 cup diced onion
- 1/4 cup diced bell pepper
- 1/4 cup diced tomato
- 1/4 cup shredded cheese
- 2 tablespoons chopped fresh cilantro
- 1 tablespoon butter or oil
- Cooking spray or butter, for greasing the griddle

Start the Griddle

1. Heat the griddle over medium heat and lightly grease it with cooking spray or butter.
2. In a small pan, melt the butter or heat the oil over medium heat. Add the chorizo and cook until it is browned and fully cooked.
3. In a small mixing bowl, beat the eggs until well scrambled.
4. Place a tortilla on the griddle and sprinkle some cheese over half of the tortilla.
5. Pour the eggs over the cheese and top with the chorizo, onion, bell pepper, tomato, and cilantro.
6. Fold the tortilla in half over the filling and press gently to seal.

7. Cook the taco for 2-3 minutes, or until the bottom is golden brown and the cheese is melted.
8. Flip the taco and cook for an additional 1-2 minutes, or until the second side is golden brown.
9. Repeat the process with the remaining tortillas and filling ingredients.
10. Serve the tacos hot, with additional toppings as desired.

Nutritional Value (Per Serving)

- Calories: 300
- Protein: 20 g
- Fat: 20 g
- Carbs: 20 g
- Fiber: 2 g
- Sugars: 4 g

Burger's Recipes

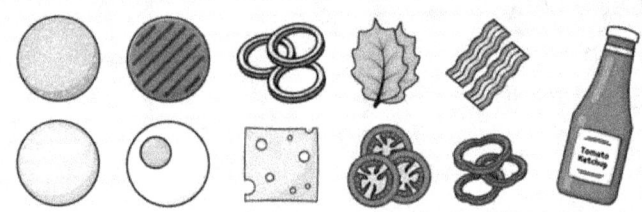

Juicy Texas Burgers

Texas-style burgers are known for their bold, hearty flavors. Made with a mixture of ground beef, spices, and diced onions, these burgers are juicy and flavorful.

Serving size: 4 burgers | Preparation time: 15 minutes

Griddling time: 10-15 minutes | Griddle temperature: 400-425°F.

Prepare Ingredients

- 1 1/2 pounds ground beef
- 1/2 cup diced onion
- 1 teaspoon ground cumin
- 1 teaspoon chili powder
- 1/2 teaspoon salt
- 1/4 teaspoon black pepper
- 4 hamburger buns
- 4 slices cheddar cheese (optional)
- Lettuce, tomato, pickles, and condiments, for serving (optional)

Start the Griddle

1. In a large mixing bowl, combine the ground beef, onion, cumin, chili powder, salt, and pepper. Mix well to combine.
2. Divide the mixture into 4 equal portions and shape each portion into a patty.
3. Place the patties on the griddle and cook for 5-6 minutes per side, or until they are cooked to your desired level of doneness.
4. During the last minute of cooking, add a slice of cheese to each patty if using.
5. Place the buns on the griddle, cut side down, and toast for 1-2 minutes, or until they are lightly toasted.
6. Assemble the burgers by placing a patty on the bottom bun and topping it with lettuce, tomato, pickles, and condiments,

if desired.
7. Serve the burgers hot, with additional toppings as desired.

Nutritional Value (Per Serving)

- Calories: 400
- Protein: 30 g
- Fat: 25 g
- Carbs: 30 g
- Fiber: 2 g
- Sugars: 4 g

Porky Burger

Made with a mixture of ground pork and beef, topped with a tangy BBQ sauce and crispy bacon, this burger is packed with flavor and moisture.

Serving size: 4 burgers | Preparation time: 15 minutes

Griddling time: 10-15 minutes to cook

Griddle temperature: 400-425°F.

Prepare Ingredients

- 1 pound ground pork
- 1/2 pound ground beef
- 1/2 cup diced onion
- 1 teaspoon ground cumin
- 1 teaspoon chili powder
- 1/2 teaspoon salt
- 1/4 teaspoon black pepper
- 4 hamburger buns
- 4 slices cheddar cheese (optional)
- 4 slices bacon, cooked until crispy
- 1/2 cup BBQ sauce
- Lettuce, tomato, pickles, and condiments, for serving (optional)

Start the Griddle

1. In a large mixing bowl, combine the ground pork, ground beef, onion, cumin, chili powder, salt, and pepper. Mix well to combine.
2. Divide the mixture into 4 equal portions and shape each portion into a patty.
3. Place the patties on the griddle and cook for 5-6 minutes per side, or until they are cooked to your desired level of doneness.

4. During the last minute of cooking, add a slice of cheese to each patty if using.
5. Place the buns on the griddle, cut side down, and toast for 1-2 minutes, or until they are lightly toasted.
6. Assemble the burgers by placing a patty on the bottom bun and topping it with BBQ sauce, bacon, lettuce, tomato, pickles, and condiments, if desired.
7. Serve the burgers hot, with additional toppings as desired.

Nutritional Value (Per Serving)

- Calories: 500
- Protein: 40 g
- Fat: 35 g
- Carbs: 30 g
- Fiber: 2 g
- Sugars: 8 g

Texas Burger with Beer Cheese Sauce

Made with a mixture of ground beef, spices, and diced onions, and topped with a creamy beer cheese sauce and served on a toasted bun, this burger is sure to become a griddle favorite.

Serving size: 4 burgers | Preparation time: 20 minutes

Griddling time: 10-15 minutes | Griddle temperature: 400-425°F

Prepare Ingredients

- 1 1/2 pounds ground beef
- 1/2 cup diced onion
- 1 teaspoon ground cumin
- 1 teaspoon chili powder
- 1/2 teaspoon salt
- 1/4 teaspoon black pepper
- 4 hamburger buns
- 4 slices cheddar cheese (optional)
- 1/2 cup beer
- 2 tablespoons butter
- 2 tablespoons all-purpose flour
- 1 cup milk
- 1/2 cup grated cheddar cheese
- Salt and pepper, to taste
- Lettuce, tomato, pickles, and condiments, for serving (optional)

Start the Griddle

1. In a large mixing bowl, combine the ground beef, onion, cumin, chili powder, salt, and pepper. Mix well to combine.
2. Divide the mixture into 4 equal portions and shape each portion into a patty.
3. Place the patties on the griddle and cook for 5-6 minutes per side, or until they are cooked to your desired level of doneness.

4. During the last minute of cooking, add a slice of cheese to each patty if using.
5. Place the buns on the griddle, cut side down, and toast for 1-2 minutes, or until they are lightly toasted.
6. While the burgers are cooking, make the beer cheese sauce. In a medium saucepan, melt the butter over medium heat. Add the flour and cook, stirring constantly, for 1-2 minutes, or until the mixture is bubbly and smooth. Slowly add the beer and milk, stirring constantly, until the mixture is smooth and thickened. Add the grated cheddar cheese and stir until it is melted. Season the sauce with salt and pepper, to taste.
7. Assemble the burgers by placing a patty on the bottom bun and topping it with beer cheese sauce, lettuce, tomato, pickles, and condiments, if desired.
8. Serve the burgers hot, with additional toppings as desired.

Nutritional Value (Per Serving)

- Calories: 500
- Protein: 30 g
- Fat: 35 g
- Carbs: 30 g
- Fiber: 2 g
- Sugars: 4 g

Homemade Veggie Burger

This Homemade Veggie Burger is made with beans, grains, and vegetables is a delicious and healthy alternative to traditional hamburgers.

Serving size: 4 burgers | Preparation time: 30 minutes

Griddling time: 10-15 minutes | Griddle temperature: 400-425°F

Prepare Ingredients

- 1 cup cooked beans (such as black beans, kidney beans, or lentils)
- 1/2 cup cooked grains (such as quinoa, brown rice, or farro)
- 1/2 cup grated vegetables (such as carrots, zucchini, or sweet potato)
- 1/4 cup chopped herbs (such as parsley, cilantro, or basil)
- 1 egg, beaten
- 2 tablespoons breadcrumbs
- 1 teaspoon ground cumin
- 1 teaspoon chili powder
- 1/2 teaspoon salt
- 1/4 teaspoon black pepper
- 4 hamburger buns
- 4 slices cheddar cheese (optional)
- Lettuce, tomato, pickles, and condiments, for serving (optional)

Start the Griddle

1. In a large mixing bowl, combine the beans, grains, vegetables, herbs, egg, breadcrumbs, cumin, chili powder, salt, and pepper. Mix well to combine.
2. Divide the mixture into 4 equal portions and shape each portion into a patty.
3. Place the patties on the griddle and cook for 5-6 minutes per side, or until they are heated through and lightly browned.

4. During the last minute of cooking, add a slice of cheese to each patty if using.
5. Place the buns on the griddle, cut side down, and toast for 1-2 minutes, or until they are lightly toasted.
6. Assemble the burgers by placing a patty on the bottom bun and topping it with lettuce, tomato, pickles, and condiments, if desired.
7. Serve the burgers hot, with additional toppings as desired.

Nutritional Value (Per Serving)

- Calories: 300
- Protein: 15 g
- Fat: 10 g
- Carbs: 45 g
- Fiber: 10 g
- Sugars: 6 g

St. Louis Gerber Pork Burger

This St. Louis Gerber Pork Burger is a unique and flavorful twist on the classic hamburger. Topped with a spicy sauce and served on a toasted bun, this burger is sure to become a griddle favorite.

Serving size: 4 burgers | Preparation time: 20 minutes

Griddling time: 10-15 minutes | Griddle temperature: 400-425°F

Prepare Ingredients

- 1 1/2 pounds ground pork
- 1/2 cup diced onion
- 1 teaspoon ground cumin
- 1 teaspoon chili powder
- 1/2 teaspoon salt
- 1/4 teaspoon black pepper
- 4 hamburger buns
- 4 slices pepper jack cheese (optional)
- 1/2 cup mayonnaise
- 1 tablespoon hot sauce
- 2 teaspoons Worcestershire sauce
- 1 teaspoon paprika
- 1/2 teaspoon garlic powder
- Lettuce, tomato, pickles, and condiments, for serving (optional)

Start the Griddle

1. In a large mixing bowl, combine the ground pork, onion, cumin, chili powder, salt, and pepper. Mix well to combine.
2. Divide the mixture into 4 equal portions and shape each portion into a patty.
3. Place the patties on the griddle and cook for 5-6 minutes per side, or until they are cooked to your desired level of doneness.
4. During the last minute of cooking, add a slice of cheese to

each patty if using.
5. Place the buns on the griddle, cut side down, and toast for 1-2 minutes, or until they are lightly toasted.
6. While the burgers are cooking, make the sauce by mixing the mayonnaise, hot sauce, Worcestershire sauce, paprika, and garlic powder in a small bowl.
7. Assemble the burgers by placing a patty on the bottom bun and topping it with sauce, lettuce, tomato, pickles, and condiments, if desired.
8. Serve the burgers hot, with additional toppings as desired.

Nutritional Value (Per Serving)

- Calories: 500
- Protein: 30 g
- Fat: 35 g
- Carbs: 30 g
- Fiber: 2 g
- Sugars: 4 g

White Cheddar Turkey Smash Burger with Apple Slaw

This Smash Burger is made with ground turkey and topped with a creamy apple slaw and is a healthy twist on the classic hamburger.

Serving size: 4 burgers | Preparation time: 30 minutes

Griddling time: 10-15 minutes | Griddle temperature: 400-425°F

Prepare Ingredients

- 1 1/2 pounds ground turkey
- 1/2 teaspoon salt
- 1/4 teaspoon black pepper
- 4 hamburger buns
- 4 slices white cheddar cheese
- 1/2 cup mayonnaise
- 1/4 cup sour cream
- 2 tablespoons apple cider vinegar
- 1 teaspoon sugar
- 1/2 teaspoon celery seed
- 4 cups shredded cabbage
- 1 apple, thinly sliced
- Lettuce, tomato, pickles, and condiments, for serving (optional)

Start the Griddle

1. In a large mixing bowl, combine the ground turkey, salt, and pepper. Mix well to combine.
2. Divide the mixture into 4 equal portions and shape each portion into a patty.
3. Place the patties on the griddle and cook for 5-6 minutes per side, or until they are cooked to your desired level of doneness.
4. During the last minute of cooking, add a slice of cheese to

each patty.
5. Place the buns on the griddle, cut side down, and toast for 1-2 minutes, or until they are lightly toasted.
6. While the burgers are cooking, make the slaw by mixing the mayonnaise, sour cream, apple cider vinegar, sugar, and celery seed in a large bowl. Add the cabbage and apple to the bowl and mix until well coated.
7. Assemble the burgers by placing a patty on the bottom bun and topping it with slaw, lettuce, tomato, pickles, and condiments, if desired.
8. Serve the burgers hot, with additional toppings as desired.

Nutritional Value (Per Serving)

- Calories: 400
- Protein: 30 g
- Fat: 25 g
- Carbs: 30 g
- Fiber: 4 g
- Sugars: 8 g

Vegetables & Side dishes

Bacon and Corn Griddle Cakes

Made with a combination of bacon, corn, and flour, these cakes are packed with flavor, but I would recommend you to top them with syrup and give your taste buds and belly a party.

Serving size: 8 cakes | Preparation time: 30 minutes

Griddling time: 10-15 minutes | Griddle temperature: 350-375°F

Prepare Ingredients

- 1 cup all-purpose flour
- 1 cup cornmeal
- 1 tablespoon sugar
- 2 teaspoons baking powder
- 1/2 teaspoon baking soda
- 1/2 teaspoon salt
- 1 cup buttermilk
- 1 egg
- 2 tablespoons melted butter
- 1/2 cup cooked and crumbled bacon
- 1/2 cup canned corn, drained
- Cooking spray or butter, for greasing the griddle
- Maple syrup and butter, for serving (optional)

Start the Griddle

1. In a large mixing bowl, combine the flour, cornmeal, sugar, baking powder, baking soda, and salt. Mix well to combine.
2. In a separate bowl, whisk together the buttermilk, egg, and melted butter.
3. Add the wet ingredients to the dry ingredients and mix until just combined. Stir in the bacon and corn.
4. Heat the griddle over medium heat and grease it with cooking spray or butter.
5. Use a 1/4 cup measuring cup to scoop the batter onto the griddle. Cook the cakes for 2-3 minutes per side, or until they

are golden brown and cooked through.
6. Serve the cakes warm, with maple syrup and butter, if desired.

Nutritional Value (Per Serving)

- Calories: 300
- Protein: 10 g
- Fat: 15 g
- Carbs: 30 g
- Fiber: 2 g
- Sugars: 8 g

Hibachi Vegetables

This a delicious and healthy side dish that can be made quickly on a gas griddle. It's sweet and savory and makes a great addition to a dinner party menu.

Serving size: 4 people | Preparation time: 20 minutes

Griddling time: 15-20 minutes | Griddle temperature: 400-450°F

Prepare Ingredients

- 1 red bell pepper, sliced
- 1 yellow bell pepper, sliced
- 1 onion, sliced
- 2 cups mushrooms, sliced
- 2 tablespoons vegetable oil
- 2 tablespoons soy sauce
- 2 tablespoons sake (or dry white wine)
- 1 tablespoon sugar
- 2 cloves garlic, minced
- Salt and pepper, to taste
- Green onions, thinly sliced, for garnish (optional)

Start the Griddle

1. In a large mixing bowl, toss the bell peppers, onions, and mushrooms with the vegetable oil, soy sauce, sake, sugar, garlic, salt, and pepper until well coated.
2. Preheat the gas griddle over medium-high heat.
3. Add the vegetables to the griddle and cook, stirring occasionally, until they are tender and lightly charred, about 15-20 minutes.
4. Remove the vegetables from the griddle, place them in a serving dish and garnish with sliced green onions, if desired.
5. Serve the vegetables warm as a side dish to any entree, or with some rice and/or a protein source such as chicken, beef, or shrimp.

Nutritional Value (Per Serving)

- Calories: 100
- Protein: 3 g
- Fat: 8 g
- Carbs: 7 g
- Fiber: 2 g
- Sugars: 4 g

Griddle Vegetable Quesadillas

These griddle vegetables are a delicious and healthy twist on traditional quesadillas. Made with a combination of vegetables, cheese, and tortillas, these quesadillas are packed with flavor and have a crispy, golden-brown exterior. They are perfect for a quick lunch or dinner.

Serving size: 4 quesadillas | Preparation time: 20 minutes

Griddling time: 10-15 minutes | Griddle temperature: 400-425°F

Prepare Ingredients

- 4 large flour tortillas
- 1 cup grated cheese (cheddar, Monterey Jack or a combination)
- 1 red bell pepper, diced
- 1 green bell pepper, diced
- 1 red onion, diced
- 1 zucchini, diced
- 1 teaspoon chili powder
- 1/2 teaspoon cumin
- Salt and pepper, to taste
- Cooking spray or butter, for greasing the griddle
- Sour cream and salsa, for serving (optional)

Start the Griddle

1. Heat the gas griddle to medium-high heat and grease it with cooking spray or butter.
2. In a bowl, mix together the bell peppers, onion, zucchini, chili powder, cumin, salt, and pepper.
3. Place a tortilla on the griddle. Sprinkle a little bit of cheese in the middle of the tortilla then add some of the vegetable mixtures. Sprinkle more cheese over top. Place another tortilla on top of that, and press down a bit to seal it.
4. Cook the quesadilla for 2-3 minutes per side, or until the tortilla is golden brown and the cheese is melted.

5. Repeat with the remaining tortillas, vegetables, and cheese.
6. Cut the quesadillas into wedges and serve warm, with sour cream and salsa, if desired.

Nutritional Value (Per Serving)

- Calories: 300
- Protein: 12 g
- Fat: 15 g
- Carbs: 25 g
- Fiber: 2 g
- Sugars: 4 g

Maple Bacon Brussels Sprouts

This delicious and unique side dish that can be made quickly on a gas griddle and is one dish that I think everyone needs to experience in their lifetime.

Serving size: 4 people | Preparation time: 20 minutes

Griddling time: 15-20 minutes | Griddle temperature: 425-450°F

Prepare Ingredients

- 1 lb. Brussels sprouts, halved
- 6-8 slices of bacon, cut into small pieces
- 2 tablespoons olive oil
- 2 tablespoons maple syrup
- Salt and pepper, to taste

Start the Griddle

1. Preheat the gas griddle to medium-high heat.
2. In a mixing bowl, toss the Brussels sprouts and bacon with olive oil, maple syrup, salt, and pepper until well coated.
3. Add the mixture to the griddle and cook, stirring occasionally, until the Brussels sprouts are tender and the bacon is crispy about 15-20 minutes.
4. Serve the Brussels sprouts warm as a side dish or as a topping for a salad.

Nutritional Value (Per Serving)

- Calories: 180
- Protein: 6 g
- Fat: 13 g
- Carbs: 12 g
- Fiber: 4 g
- Sugars: 7 g

Crispy Fried Green Tomatoes

This southern classic is made with green tomatoes that are breaded and fried to perfection, resulting in a crispy exterior and a tangy, juicy interior.

Serving size: 4 people | Preparation time: 30 minutes

Griddling time: 15-20 minutes | Griddle temperature: 375-400°F

Prepare Ingredients

- 4-6 green tomatoes, sliced 1/4 inch thick
- 1/2 cup all-purpose flour
- 1/2 teaspoon paprika
- 1/4 teaspoon cayenne pepper
- Salt and pepper, to taste
- 2 eggs, beaten
- 1 cup breadcrumbs
- 1 cup cornmeal
- Vegetable oil, for frying
- Ranch dressing, for serving (optional)

Start the Griddle

1. In a shallow dish, combine the flour, paprika, cayenne pepper, salt and pepper.
2. In a second shallow dish, beat the eggs.
3. In a third shallow dish, combine the breadcrumbs and cornmeal.
4. Dip the tomato slices in the flour mixture, then the eggs, and then coat them well in the breadcrumb mixture.
5. Heat the oil in the gas griddle to 375-400°F. Carefully place the breaded tomatoes in the griddle and fry them for 2-3 minutes on each side, or until they are golden brown.
6. Remove the tomatoes from the griddle with a slotted spoon and place them on a papertowel-lined plate to drain.
7. Serve the tomatoes warm with ranch dressing, if desi red.

Nutritional Value (Per Serving)

- Calories: 260
- Protein: 7 g
- Fat: 14 g
- Carbs: 27 g
- Fiber: 3 g
- Sugars: 10 g

Griddled Vegetables with Melting Aubergines

This flavorful and healthy dish that is is packed with vitamins, minerals and antioxidants and is perfect for a summer meal or as a side dish.

Serving size: 4 people | Preparation time: 15 minutes

Griddling time: 15-20 minutes | Griddle temperature: 375-400°F

Prepare Ingredients
- 1 large aubergine, sliced
- 1 red pepper, sliced
- 1 yellow pepper, sliced
- 1 courgette, sliced
- 1 red onion, sliced
- 1 tbsp olive oil
- 1 tsp smoked paprika
- 1 tsp dried oregano
- 1 tsp garlic powder
- Salt and pepper, to taste
- 1 tbsp chopped fresh parsley

Start the Griddle
1. Preheat the gas griddle to 375-400°F.
2. In a large bowl, combine the aubergine, red pepper, yellow pepper, courgette, and red onion.
3. Add the olive oil, smoked paprika, oregano, garlic powder, salt, and pepper. Toss the vegetables to coat them evenly.
4. Place the vegetables on the griddle and cook for 8-10 minutes per side or until tender and charred.
5. Remove the vegetables from the griddle and sprinkle them with the fresh parsley.
6. Serve the vegetables hot or at room temperature as a side dish or as a topping for pasta, rice, or quinoa.

Nutritional Value (Per Serving)

- Calories: 120
- Protein: 2g
- Fat: 8g
- Carbs: 12g
- Fiber: 3g
- Sugars: 7g

Beef Recipes

Flash-Marinated Skirt Steak

This recipe marinates the steak for only a short period of time to add flavor and tenderize the meat.

Serving size: 4 people | Preparation time: 15 minutes

Marination time: 15 minutes | Griddling time: 10-15 minutes

Griddle temperature: 425-450°F

Prepare Ingredients

- 1 1/2 lb. skirt steak
- 1/4 cup soy sauce
- 2 tablespoons olive oil
- 2 cloves of garlic, minced
- 1 tablespoon brown sugar
- 1 teaspoon smoked paprika
- 1/4 teaspoon cayenne pepper
- Salt and pepper, to taste

Start the Griddle

1. In a shallow dish, mix together the soy sauce, olive oil, garlic, brown sugar, smoked paprika, cayenne pepper, salt, and pepper.
2. Place the steak in the dish and coat it well with the marinade. Allow the steak to marinate for 15 minutes.
3. Heat the gas griddle to 425-450°F.
4. Remove the steak from the marinade and discard the marinade.
5. Place the steak on the griddle and cook it for 4-5 minutes per side, or until it reaches your desired level of doneness.
6. Let the steak rest for 5-10 minutes before slicing it against the grain.
7. Serve the steak with your favorite sides or toppings.

Nutritional Value (Per Serving)

- Calories: 330
- Protein: 45 g
- Fat: 14 g
- Carbs: 4 g
- Fiber: 1 g
- Sugars: 3 g

Homemade Meatballs

This recipe for meatballs is made with a combination of ground beef and pork, seasoned with classic Italian herbs and spices, and cooked to perfection on a gas griddle.

Serving size: 6 people | Preparation time: 15 minutes

Griddling time: 15-20 minutes | Griddle temperature: 425-450°F

Prepare Ingredients

- 1 lb. ground beef
- 1 lb. ground pork
- 1/2 cup breadcrumbs
- 1/4 cup grated Parmesan cheese
- 1/4 cup minced onion
- 2 cloves of garlic, minced
- 2 eggs
- 1 tablespoon chopped fresh parsley
- 1 teaspoon dried basil
- 1 teaspoon dried oregano
- 1/2 teaspoon salt
- 1/4 teaspoon pepper

Start the Griddle

1. In a large mixing bowl, combine the ground beef, ground pork, breadcrumbs, Parmesan cheese, onion, garlic, eggs, parsley, basil, oregano, salt, and pepper. Mix until well combined.
2. Shape the mixture into 1 and 1/2-inch meatballs.
3. Heat the gas griddle to 425-450°F.
4. Place the meatballs on the griddle and cook for 10-12 minutes, turning them occasionally, until they are browned and cooked through.
5. Serve the meatballs warm with spaghetti and marinara sauce or in a sandwich or as an appetizer.

Nutritional Value (Per Serving)

- Calories: 400
- Protein: 25 g
- Fat: 29 g
- Carbs: 15 g
- Fiber: 1 g
- Sugars: 2 g

Copycat Texas Roadhouse Steak

This copycat recipe captures the bold flavors of the steaks served at Texas Roadhouse restaurants. It's a juicy, flavorful steak that is sure to satisfy any steak lover.

Service size: 4 people | Preparation time: 15 minutes

Marination time: 15 minutes | Griddling time: 10-15 minutes

Griddle temperature: 425-450°

F Prepare Ingredients

- 4 (8-ounce) beef steaks (such as ribeye, sirloin, or New York strip)
- 2 tablespoons paprika
- 2 tablespoons brown sugar
- 2 tablespoons salt
- 1 tablespoon black pepper
- 1 tablespoon garlic powder
- 1 tablespoon onion powder
- 1 tablespoon dried thyme
- 1 teaspoon cayenne pepper
- 2 tablespoons vegetable oil

Start the Griddle

1. Mix together the paprika, brown sugar, salt, pepper, garlic powder, onion powder, thyme, and cayenne pepper in a small bowl.
2. Rub the mixture all over the steaks and let them sit at room temperature for 15 minutes.
3. Heat the oil on the gas griddle to 425-450°F.
4. Place the steaks on the griddle and cook them for 4-5 minutes per side, or until they reach your desired level of doneness.
5. Remove the steaks from the griddle and let them rest for 5-10 minutes before slicing and serving.

Nutritional Value (Per Serving)

- Calories: 600
- Protein: 60g
- Fat: 40g
- Carbs: 10g
- Fiber: 3g
- Sugars: 5g

Griddle Steak Bites

These steak bites are marinated in a flavorful mix of soy sauce, brown sugar, garlic, and spices before they are cooked on a hot gas griddle.

Serving size: 6 people | Preparation time: 10 minutes

Marination time: 2 hours | Griddling time: 8-10 minutes

Griddle temperature: 425-450°F

Prepare Ingredients

- 2 lbs. sirloin steak, cut into 1-inch cubes
- 1/2 cup soy sauce
- 1/4 cup brown sugar
- 2 cloves of garlic, minced
- 1 teaspoon smoked paprika
- 1/2 teaspoon onion powder
- 1/4 teaspoon black pepper
- 1/4 teaspoon cayenne pepper
- Vegetable oil, for frying

Start the Griddle

1. In a large bowl, mix together the soy sauce, brown sugar, garlic, smoked paprika, onion powder, black pepper, and cayenne pepper.
2. Add the steak cubes to the marinade and toss to coat. Cover and refrigerate for at least 2 hours.
3. Heat the oil on the gas griddle to 425-450°F.
4. Drain the steak from the marinade and discard the marinade.
5. Carefully place the steak bites on the griddle and cook them for 2-3 minutes per side, or until they are browned and cooked through.
6. Remove the steak bites from the griddle and let them rest for a few minutes before serving.

Nutritional Value (Per Serving)

- Calories: 480
- Protein: 50g
- Fat: 24g
- Carbs: 12g
- Fiber: 1g
- Sugars: 8g

Grilled Beef Tenderloin with Herb-Garlic-Pepper Coating

This recipe for Grilled Beef Tenderloin with Herb-Garlic-Pepper Coating is a delicious way to enjoy a tender and juicy cut of beef.

Serving size: 6 people | Preparation time: 15 minutes

Marination time: 2 hours | Griddling time: 20-25 minutes

Griddle temperature: 425-450°F

Prepare Ingredients

- 2 lbs. beef tenderloin, trimmed
- 2 cloves of garlic, minced
- 2 tablespoons olive oil
- 1 tablespoon fresh rosemary, finely chopped
- 1 tablespoon fresh thyme, finely chopped
- 1 tablespoon fresh parsley, finely chopped
- 1 teaspoon salt
- 1/2 teaspoon black pepper
- additional oil for griddling

Start the Griddle

1. In a small bowl, mix together the garlic, olive oil, rosemary, thyme, parsley, salt, and pepper.
2. Rub the mixture all over the beef tenderloin, cover, and refrigerate for at least 2 hours.
3. Heat the oil on the gas griddle to 425-450°F.
4. Place the beef tenderloin on the griddle and cook it for 10-12 minutes per side or until it reaches the desired level of doneness.
5. Remove the beef tenderloin from the griddle and let it rest for 5-10 minutes before slicing and serving.

Nutritional Value (Per Serving)

- Calories: 400
- Protein: 40g
- Fat: 20g
- Carbs: 2g
- Fiber: 1g
- Sugars: 0g

Sirloin Wrapped Jalapeño Poppers

This is a fun and flavorful way to enjoy jalapeño poppers, with a juicy and tender sirloin steak wrapping them, with a cream filling.

Serving size: 8 people | Preparation time: 20 minutes

Griddling time: 15-20 minutes | Griddle temperature: 425-450°F

Prepare Ingredients

- 8 jalapeño peppers, halved and seeded
- 8 oz cream cheese, softened
- 8 strips of bacon, sliced in half
- 8 sirloin steaks, pounded thin
- Salt and pepper, to taste
- Vegetable oil, for griddling

Start the Griddle

1. Preheat the gas griddle to 425-450°F.
2. In a bowl, mix together the cream cheese with salt and pepper to taste.
3. Stuff the jalapeño halves with the cream cheese mixture.
4. Wrap a half strip of bacon around each jalapeño popper and secure it with a toothpick.
5. Place the poppers on the griddle and cook them for 8-10 minutes or until the bacon is crispy and the poppers are heated through.
6. Season the sirloin steaks with salt and pepper, then griddle them to your desired doneness.
7. Carefully wrap the steak around the jalapeño popper and toothpick it to secure it.
8. Griddle the wrapped poppers for 2-3 minutes on each side, or until the steak is browned and cooked through.

Nutritional Value (Per Serving)

- Calories: 550

- Protein: 45g
- Fat: 40g
- Carbs: 5g
- Fiber: 1g
- Sugars: 3g

Pork Recipes

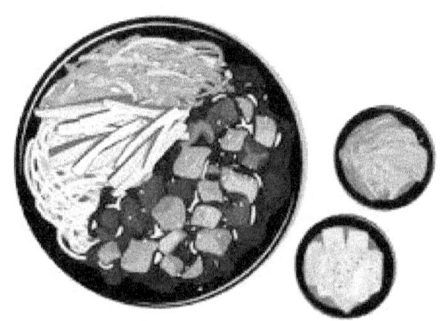

Perfect Pork Chops

The pork chops are seasoned with garlic, thyme, and rosemary, then grilled to perfection and if you want to add some extra flavor you can add some marinade. Get creative!

Serving size: 4 people | Preparation time: 15 minutes

Griddling time: 8-10 minutes | Griddle temperature: 425-450°F

Prepare Ingredients

- 4 bone-in pork chops, about 1-inch thick
- Salt and pepper, to taste
- 2 cloves of garlic, minced
- 1 tbsp olive oil
- 1 tsp dried thyme
- 1 tsp dried rosemary

Start the Griddle

1. Preheat the gas griddle to 425-450°F.
2. Season the pork chops with salt, pepper, minced garlic, thyme, and rosemary.
3. Brush the pork chops with olive oil on both sides.
4. Place the pork chops on the griddle and cook them for 4-5 minutes per side or until the internal temperature reaches 145°F.
5. Let the pork chops rest for 5 minutes before slicing or serving.

Nutritional Value (Per Serving)

- Calories: 340
- Protein: 40g
- Fat: 25g
- Carbs: 1g
- Fiber: 0g
- Sugars: 0g

★ ★ ★ ★ ★

Smoky Grilled Pork Chops

The marinade with brown sugar, smoked paprika, garlic powder, and apple cider vinegar gives the pork a special flavor, and grilling gives the pork a crispy exterior while keeping it moist inside.

Serving size: 4 people | Preparation time: 30 minutes (plus marinating time) | Griddling time: 8-10 minutes

Griddle temperature: 425-450°F

Prepare Ingredients

- 4 bone-in pork chops, about 1-inch thick
- 1/4 cup brown sugar
- 2 tablespoons smoked paprika
- 1 tablespoon garlic powder
- 1 teaspoon salt
- 1 teaspoon black pepper
- 1/4 cup olive oil
- 1/4 cup apple cider vinegar

Start the Griddle

1. In a small bowl, mix together brown sugar, smoked paprika, garlic powder, salt, and pepper.
2. In another small bowl, mix together the olive oil and apple cider vinegar.
3. Place the pork chops in a shallow dish and pour the marinade over them, making sure to coat them evenly. Cover and refrigerate for at least 2 hours or overnight for best results.
4. Preheat the gas griddle to 425-450°F.
5. Remove the pork chops from the marinade and let any excess marinade drip off.
6. Place the pork chops on the griddle and cook them for 4-5 minutes per side or until the internal temperature reaches 145°F.
7. Let the pork chops rest for 5 minutes before slicing or serving.

Nutritional Value (Per Serving)

- Calories: 400
- Protein: 40g
- Fat: 25g
- Carbs: 15g
- Fiber: 1g
- Sugars: 13g

Marinated Pork Skewers

Marinating the pork in a mixture of soy sauce, brown sugar, garlic, ginger, sesame oil, and red pepper flakes, and grilling the skewers will give it a nice crust on the outside and juicy on the inside.

Serving size: 4 people |Preparation time: 30 minutes (plus marinating time) | Griddling time: 10-12 minutes

Griddle temperature: 425-450°F

Prepare Ingredients

- 1 lb pork tenderloin, cut into 1-inch cubes
- 1/4 cup soy sauce
- 1/4 cup brown sugar
- 2 cloves of garlic, minced
- 1 tbsp olive oil
- 1 tsp ground ginger
- 1 tsp sesame oil
- 1/4 tsp red pepper flakes (optional)
- wooden skewers (soaked in water for at least 30 minutes before using)

Start the Griddle

1. In a small bowl, mix together soy sauce, brown sugar, minced garlic, olive oil, ground ginger, sesame oil, and red pepper flakes (if using).
2. Place the pork cubes in a shallow dish and pour the marinade over them, making sure to coat them evenly. Cover and refrigerate for at least 2 hours, or overnight for best results.
3. Preheat the gas griddle to 425-450°F.
4. Thread the pork cubes onto the skewers, leaving a little space between each piece.
5. Place the skewers on the griddle and cook them for 5-6 minutes per side, or until the pork is cooked through and the internal temperature reaches 145°F.

6. Let the skewers rest for a few minutes before serving.

Nutritional Value (Per Serving)

- Calories: 200
- Protein: 20g
- Fat: 10g
- Carbs: 12g
- Fiber: 0g
- Sugars: 10g

Griddled Pork And Peaches

This recipe gives you a combination of sweet and savory flavors, by marinating the pork medallions with honey, Dijon mustard and thyme, and then griddle it.

Serving size: 4 people | Preparation time: 20 minutes

Griddling time: 8-10 minutes | Griddle temperature: 425-450°F

Prepare Ingredients

- 1 lb pork tenderloin, sliced into 1/2-inch thick medallions
- Salt and pepper, to taste
- 2 tbsp olive oil
- 4 ripe peaches, cut into wedges
- 1 tbsp honey
- 1 tsp Dijon mustard
- 1 tbsp chopped fresh thyme

Start the Griddle

1. Season the pork medallions with salt and pepper on both sides.
2. Heat the olive oil in a gas griddle over medium-high heat.
3. Add the pork medallions and cook for 4-5 minutes per side or until the internal temperature reaches 145°F.
4. Remove the pork from the griddle and set it aside to rest.
5. In the same griddle, add the peach wedges, honey, Dijon mustard, and thyme.
6. Cook for 23 minutes or until the peaches are slightly softened and caramelized.
7. Serve the pork medallions with the peaches on top.
8. Enjoy!

Nutritional Value (Per Serving)

- Calories: 300
- Protein: 30g
- Fat: 15g

- Carbs: 15g
- Fiber: 3g
- Sugars: 12g

Griddle Pork Fried Rice

The pork is seasoned with salt and pepper and cooked on a gas griddle until and then mixed with onions, garlic, cooked rice, soy sauce, eggs, frozen peas and carrots, and green onions–this dish can't go wrong.

Serving size: 4 people | Preparation time: 20 minutes

Griddling time: 15-20 minutes | Griddle temperature: 425-450°F

Prepare Ingredients

- 1 lb pork tenderloin, diced
- 1 tsp salt
- 1 tsp pepper
- 1 tbsp vegetable oil
- 1 onion, diced
- 2 cloves of garlic, minced
- 2 cups cooked white rice
- 1/4 cup soy sauce
- 2 eggs, beaten
- 1 cup frozen peas and carrots
- 2 green onions, sliced

Start the Griddle

1. Season the pork with salt and pepper.
2. Heat the vegetable oil in a gas griddle over medium-high heat. Add the pork and cook for 6-8 minutes or until the internal temperature reaches 145°F.
3. Remove the pork from the griddle and set it aside.
4. In the same griddle, add the onion and garlic and cook until softened.
5. Add the cooked rice, soy sauce, eggs, peas and carrots, and green onions. Cook for an additional 3-4 minutes, or until the eggs are fully cooked.
6. Add the pork back to the griddle, and cook for 1-2 minutes to heat it through.

Nutritional Value (Per Serving)

- Calories: 400
- Protein: 30g
- Fat: 15g
- Carbs: 40g
- Fiber: 3g
- Sugars: 3g

Simple Smoked Pulled Pork Butt

This recipe allows you to achieve that traditional barbecue style pulled pork, by smoking it on a gas griddle, which allows the pork to cook until it's perfectly tender and juicy.

Serving size: 8 people | Preparation time: 20 minutes (plus smoking time) | Smoking time: 3-4 hours | Griddling time: 2-3 hours

Griddle temperature: 250-275°F

Prepare Ingredients

- 1 (8-10 lb) pork butt
- 1 cup of your favorite BBQ rub
- 1 cup of apple juice

Start the Griddle

1. Trim any excess fat from the pork butt.
2. Rub the pork butt evenly with the BBQ rub.
3. Place the pork butt in a large aluminum pan and pour apple juice over it.
4. Cover the pan with foil and let it sit in the refrigerator for at least 4 hours or overnight for best results.
5. Preheat your gas griddle to 250-275°F.
6. Place the pork butt on the griddle and smoke it with your preferred smoking wood for 3-4 hours or until the internal temperature reaches 205°F.
7. Smoking on a gas griddle is more challenging than using a traditional smoker, and will not produce the same level of smoke flavor and complexity that you can get from traditional smoking (it is also important to make sure that you're using a gas griddle that is capable of handling the low temperatures and that can hold the wood chips, or a smoke box if possible). But here is how you can smoke using a griddle.
    a. **Add wood chips or chunks:** You will need to add wood chips or chunks to the griddle in order to achieve a smoky

flavor. Soak the wood chips in water for at least 30 minutes before adding them to the griddle.

b. **Create a smoke box:** You can create a smoke box by placing the soaked wood chips in a foil pouch and then placing the pouch on the griddle. This will allow the wood chips to smoke without catching fire.

c. **Keep the griddle closed:** Try to keep the lid of the griddle closed as much as possible to trap the smoke inside and give your food a chance to absorb the smoky flavor.

d. **Lower the temperature:** It's important to keep the temperature low and steady, around 250-275°F, during the smoking process. This will help ensure that the meat cooks slowly and has a chance to absorb the smoke flavor.

e. **Add a thermometer:** Keep an eye on the internal temperature of your meat to ensure it reaches the desired level of doneness.

8. Remove the pork from the griddle and let it rest for 30 minutes.
9. Shred the pork with two forks or meat claws and serve with your favorite BBQ sauce.

Nutritional Value (Per Serving)

- Calories: 450
- Protein: 50g
- Fat: 30g
- Carbs: 5g
- Fiber: 1g
- Sugars: 3g

Chicken Recipes

Seared Chicken Breasts

This is a simple and easy recipe for juicy and flavorful chicken breasts. The searing will give you a nice crust on the outside while keeping the chicken moist inside.

Serving size: 4 people | Preparation time: 10 minutes

Griddling time: 6-8 minutes | Griddle temperature: 425-450°F

Prepare Ingredients

- 4 boneless, skinless chicken breasts
- 1 tsp salt
- 1 tsp pepper
- 1 tbsp olive oil

Start the Griddle

1. Season both sides of the chicken breasts with salt and pepper.
2. Heat the olive oil in a gas griddle over medium-high heat.
3. Place the chicken breasts on the griddle and cook for 3-4 minutes per side, or until the internal temperature reaches 165°F.
4. Remove the chicken from the griddle and let it rest for a few minutes before serving.

Nutritional Value (Per Serving)

- Calories: 200
- Protein: 30g
- Fat: 8g
- Carbs: 0g
- Fiber: 0g
- Sugars: 0g

Chicken Teriyaki

This recipe for Chicken Teriyaki is a classic Japanese dish with a sweet soy sauce marinade. It's simple and elegant, it's Japanese food.

Serving size: 4 people | Preparation time: 10 minutes

Griddling time: 6-8 minutes | Griddle temperature: 425-450°F

Prepare Ingredients

- 4 boneless, skinless chicken breasts
- 1/2 cup soy sauce
- 1/2 cup mirin (Japanese sweet rice wine)
- 1/4 cup sake (optional)
- 1/4 cup brown sugar
- 1 tbsp grated ginger
- 1 tsp minced garlic
- 1 tbsp vegetable oil
- 1 green onion, thinly sliced (for garnish)
- 1 tbsp corn starch dissolved in 1 tbsp cold water

Start the Griddle

1. In a bowl, mix together the soy sauce, mirin, sake (if using), brown sugar, ginger, and garlic.
2. Place the chicken breasts in a large resealable plastic bag and pour the marinade over the chicken. Seal the bag and toss to evenly coat the chicken. Marinate in the refrigerator for at least 2 hours, or overnight for best results.
3. Heat the vegetable oil in a gas griddle over medium-high heat.
4. Remove the chicken from the marinade, shaking off any excess liquid. Place the chicken on the griddle and discard the remaining marinade.
5. Cook the chicken for 3-4 minutes per side, or until the internal temperature reaches 165°F.
6. While the chicken is cooking, reduce the marinade in a small saucepan over mediumhigh heat. Once it comes to a boil,

reduce heat to low and slowly pour the cornstarch mixture in, whisking constantly, until the sauce thickens.
7. Once the chicken is done, remove it from the griddle, place it on a plate or cutting board and let it rest for a few minutes.
8. Drizzle the thickened sauce over the chicken.
9. Garnish with green onion and serve with rice.

Nutritional Value (Per Serving)

- Calories: 250
- Protein: 30g
- Fat: 10g
- Carbs: 15g
- Fiber: 1g
- Sugars: 12g

Chicken Fried Rice

The chicken is griddled, then set aside and later tossed in with the fried rice mixture made with onion, garlic, soy sauce, eggs, peas, carrots, and green onions. Can't go wrong with this one.

Serving size: 4 people | Preparation time: 20 minutes

Griddling time: 15-20 minutes | Griddle temperature: 425-450°F

Prepare Ingredients

- 1 lb boneless, skinless chicken breasts, diced
- 1 tsp salt
- 1 tsp pepper
- 1 tbsp vegetable oil
- 1 onion, diced
- 2 cloves of garlic, minced
- 2 cups cooked white rice
- 1/4 cup soy sauce
- 2 eggs, beaten
- 1 cup frozen peas and carrots
- 2 green onions, sliced

Start the Griddle

1. Season the chicken with salt and pepper.
2. Heat the vegetable oil in a gas griddle over medium-high heat. Add the chicken and cook for 6-8 minutes or until the internal temperature reaches 165°F.
3. Remove the chicken from the griddle and set it aside.
4. In the same griddle, add the onion and garlic and cook until softened.
5. Add the cooked rice, soy sauce, eggs, peas and carrots, and green onions. Cook for an additional 3-4 minutes, or until the eggs are fully cooked.
6. Add the chicken back to the griddle, and cook for 1-2 minutes to heat it through.

Nutritional Value (Per Serving)

- Calories: 400
- Protein: 30g
- Fat: 15g
- Carbs: 40g
- Fiber: 3g
- Sugars: 3g

Perfect Chicken Wings

The wings are griddled and then tossed in your favorite wing sauce, making it a healthier option compared to deep-frying.

Serving size: 4 people | Preparation time: 10 minutes

Griddling time: 15-20 minutes | Griddle temperature: 425-450°F

Prepare Ingredients

- 2 lb chicken wings
- 1 tsp salt
- 1 tsp black pepper
- 1 tbsp vegetable oil
- Your favorite wing sauce

Start the Griddle

1. Season the chicken wings with salt and pepper.
2. Heat the vegetable oil on a gas griddle over medium-high heat.
3. Place the wings on the griddle and cook for 8-10 minutes per side or until the internal temperature reaches 165°F.
4. Remove the wings from the griddle and toss them in your favorite wing sauce.
5. Return the wings to the griddle and cook for an additional 2-3 minutes, or until the sauce is heated through and the wings are glazed.

Nutritional Value (Per Serving)

- Calories: 400
- Protein: 25g
- Fat: 30g
- Carbs: 10g
- Fiber: 1g
- Sugars: 8g

Chicken Lo Mein

This recipe is a classic Chinese dish that is easy to make on a gas griddle, the chicken is cooked on the griddle, then set aside and later added back to the dish.

Serving size: 4 people | Preparation time: 20 minutes

Griddling time: 15-20 minutes |Griddle temperature: 425-450°F

Prepare Ingredients

- 8 oz boneless, skinless chicken breasts, sliced
- 1/2 tsp salt
- 1/4 tsp pepper
- 1 tbsp vegetable oil
- 1 onion, sliced
- 1 bell pepper, sliced
- 1 cup sliced mushrooms
- 2 cloves of garlic, minced
- 2 cups cooked lo mein noodles
- 1/4 cup soy sauce
- 1/4 cup oyster sauce
- 1 tbsp rice vinegar
- 1 tsp sesame oil
- 2 green onions, sliced

Start the Griddle

1. Season the chicken with salt and pepper.
2. Heat the vegetable oil in a gas griddle over medium-high heat. Add the chicken and cook for 6-8 minutes or until the internal temperature reaches 165°F.
3. Remove the chicken from the griddle and set it aside.
4. On the same griddle, add the onion, bell pepper, mushrooms, and garlic. Cook until softened.
5. Add the cooked noodles, soy sauce, oyster sauce, rice vinegar, and sesame oil. Stir fry for an additional 2-3 minutes.

6. Add the chicken back to the griddle, and cook for 1-2 minutes to heat it through.
7. Serve the Lo Mein in bowls, garnished with green onions, and enjoy!

Nutritional Value (Per Serving)

- Calories: 400
- Protein: 20g
- Fat: 15g
- Carbs: 40g
- Fiber: 2g
- Sugars: 5g

Chicken With Mushroom Gravy

The dish is made with chicken, sautéed onion, mushrooms, garlic and thickened with a mixture of chicken broth and cornstarch with a touch of cream. It's a warm and hearty meal.

Serving size: 4 people | Preparation time: 15 minutes

Griddling time: 15-20 minutes | Griddle temperature: 425-450°F

Prepare Ingredients

- 4 boneless, skinless chicken breasts
- 1 tsp salt
- 1 tsp pepper
- 1 tbsp vegetable oil
- 1 onion, sliced
- 8 oz sliced mushrooms
- 2 cloves of garlic, minced
- 1 cup chicken broth
- 2 tbsp cornstarch
- 1/4 cup heavy cream
- 1 tbsp chopped fresh parsley (for garnish)

Start the Griddle

1. Season both sides of the chicken breasts with salt and pepper.
2. Heat the vegetable oil in a gas griddle over medium-high heat.
3. Place the chicken breasts on the griddle and cook for 6-8 minutes per side or until the internal temperature reaches 165°F.
4. Remove the chicken from the griddle and set it aside.
5. On the same griddle, add the onion, mushrooms, and garlic. Cook until softened.
6. In a small bowl, mix together the chicken broth and cornstarch.
7. Add the broth mixture and heavy cream to the griddle and stir until the sauce thickens.

8. Add the chicken back to the griddle and spoon the gravy over the top. Cook for an additional 1-2 minutes or until the chicken is heated through.
9. Serve the chicken with the gravy and garnish with parsley.

Nutritional Value (Per Serving)
- Calories: 300
- Protein: 30g
- Fat: 20g
- Carbs: 7g
- Fiber: 1g
- Sugars: 3g

Poultry Recipes

Herb Roasted Turkey

The turkey is seasoned with a blend of herbs and cooked to perfection in the griddle, which results in a juicy and flavorful turkey that is perfect for a special occasion or holiday meal.

Serving size: 8-10 people | Preparation time: 15 minutes

Griddling time: 2-3 hours |Griddle temperature: 350-375°F

Prepare Ingredients

- 1 (12-14 lb) turkey, thawed and giblets removed
- 1 tbsp olive oil
- 1 tsp salt
- 1 tsp black pepper
- 1 tbsp chopped fresh rosemary
- 1 tbsp chopped fresh thyme
- 1 tbsp chopped fresh sage 1 onion, cut into wedges
- 2 cloves of garlic, minced
- 2 cups chicken broth

Start the Griddle

1. Preheat the gas griddle to 350-375°F.
2. Rinse the turkey and pat it dry with paper towels.
3. In a small bowl, mix together the olive oil, salt, pepper, rosemary, thyme, and sage.
4. Rub the herb mixture all over the turkey.
5. Place the turkey on the griddle and add the onion and garlic.
6. Pour the chicken broth over the turkey.
7. Close the lid and cook the turkey for 2-3 hours or until the internal temperature reaches 165°F in the thickest part of the turkey.
8. Remove the turkey from the griddle and let it rest for at least 20 minutes before carving.

Nutritional Value (Per Serving)

- Calories: 400
- Protein: 30g
- Fat: 15g
- Carbs: 0g
- Fiber: 0g
- Sugars: 0g

Marinated Smoked Turkey Breast

The turkey is seasoned with salt, pepper, and BBQ rub and cooked using the indirect grilling method, which means the turkey is placed away from the heat source and the lid is closed.

Serving size: 8 people | Preparation time: 8 hours (marination)

Griddling time: 1.5-2 hours | Griddle temperature: 225-250°F

Prepare Ingredients

- 1 (6-8 lb) turkey breast, thawed and giblets removed
- 1 cup of your favorite marinade
- 1 tbsp vegetable oil
- 1 tsp salt
- 1 tsp pepper
- 1 tbsp your favorite BBQ rub

Start the Griddle

1. In a large resealable bag, combine your favorite marinade and turkey breast. Seal the bag, and refrigerate for at least 8 hours or overnight for best results.
2. Preheat the gas griddle to 225-250°F and set it up for indirect grilling.
3. Remove the turkey breast from the marinade and pat it dry with paper towels.
4. Brush the turkey breast with vegetable oil and season with salt, pepper, and BBQ rub.
5. Place the turkey breast on the griddle, away from the heat source and close the lid.
6. Cook the turkey breast for 1.5-2 hours or until the internal temperature reaches 165°F.
7. Remove the turkey breast from the griddle, and let it rest for at least 15 minutes before slicing and serving.

Nutritional Value (Per Serving)

- Calories: 250
- Protein: 40g
- Fat: 10g
- Carbs: 2g
- Fiber: 0g
- Sugars: 2g

Brined Grilled Turkey With Maple Bourbon Glaze

This dish is filled with nutrients and in addition, the maple syrup, brown sugar and soy sauce make it a sweet and savoury delight.

Serving size: 8-10 people | Preparation time: 12 hours (brining)

Griddling time: 2-3 hours | Griddle temperature: 350-375°F

Prepare Ingredients

- 1 (12-14 lb) turkey, thawed and giblets removed

For the brine:

- 2 gallons water
- 1 cup kosher salt
- 1 cup maple syrup
- 1 cup brown sugar
- 1 cup soy sauce
- 1 cup bourbon
- 1 tbsp black peppercorns
- 1 tbsp juniper berries
- 1 tbsp chopped fresh rosemary
- 1 tbsp chopped fresh thyme
- 1 tbsp chopped fresh sage
- 1 onion, cut into wedges
- 2 cloves of garlic, minced

For the glaze:

- 1/2 cup maple syrup
- 1/4 cup bourbon
- 1 tbsp Dijon mustard
- 1 tsp chopped fresh rosemary
- 1 tsp chopped fresh thyme
- 1 tsp chopped fresh sage

Start the Griddle

1. In a large pot, combine the water, kosher salt, maple syrup, brown sugar, soy sauce, bourbon, peppercorns, juniper berries, rosemary, thyme, and sage. Bring the mixture to a boil, then remove it from the heat and let it cool to room temperature.
2. Place the turkey in a large brining bag or a large pot and pour the cooled brine over the turkey. Seal the bag or cover the pot and refrigerate for at least 12 hours or overnight.
3. Preheat the gas griddle to 350-375°F.
4. Remove the turkey from the brine and pat it dry with paper towels.
5. In a small pot, combine the maple syrup, bourbon, mustard, rosemary, thyme, and sage. Bring the mixture to a simmer and cook for 2-3 minutes or until thickened.
6. Place the turkey on the griddle and brush it with the glaze. Close the lid and cook the turkey for 2-3 hours or until the internal temperature reaches 165°F in the thickest part of the turkey.
7. Remove the turkey from the griddle and let it rest for at least 20 minutes before serving.

Nutritional Value (Per Serving)

- Caloric content: 400-500 calories
- Protein: 30-35 grams
- Fat: 20-25 grams
- Carbohydrates: 20-25 grams
- Fiber: 1-2 grams
- Sugar: 15-20 grams
- Sodium: 600-700 mg

Lamb Recipes

Griddled Lamb With Spiced New Potatoes

The lamb is seasoned with a flavorful spice blend, while the new potatoes are tossed with the same spice blend and cooked along the lamb to make a satisfying and well-rounded meal.

Serving size: 4 people | Preparation time: 15 minutes

Griddling time: 15-20 minutes | Griddle temperature: 400-450°F

Prepare Ingredients

For the lamb:

- 1 lb lamb leg steaks
- 1 tsp ground cumin
- 1 tsp ground coriander
- 1 tsp ground turmeric
- 1 tsp smoked paprika
- 1 tsp salt
- 1 tsp black pepper
- 1 tbsp olive oil

For the potatoes:

- 1 lb new potatoes washed and halved
- 1 tbsp olive oil
- 1 tsp ground cumin
- 1 tsp ground coriander
- 1 tsp ground turmeric
- 1 tsp smoked paprika
- 1 tsp salt
- 1 tsp black pepper

Start the Griddle

1. Preheat the gas griddle to 400-450°F.
2. In a small bowl, mix together the cumin, coriander, turmeric,

paprika, salt, and pepper.
3. Rub the lamb steaks with the spice mixture and olive oil.
4. In another small bowl, mix together the cumin, coriander, turmeric, paprika, salt, and pepper. Toss the potatoes with the mixture and olive oil.
5. Place the lamb steaks and potatoes on the griddle and cook for 7-8 minutes on each side or until the lamb is cooked to your desired doneness and the potatoes are browned and tender.
6. Serve the lamb steaks and spiced potatoes hot.

Nutritional Value (Per Serving)
- Caloric content: 350-400 calories
- Protein: 30-35 grams
- Fat: 15-20 grams
- Carbohydrates: 30-35 grams
- Fiber: 5 grams
- Sugar: 2 grams
- Vitamin B12: good source
- Iron: good source
- Zinc: good source
- Vitamin B6: good source
- Vitamin C: good source
- Potassium: good source

Garlic Butter Lamb Chops

This is a delicious and easy-to-make recipe that is perfect for a special occasion or a weeknight dinner. The recipe can be easily made on a gas griddle.

Serving size: 4 people | Preparation time: 10 minutes

Griddling time: 10-15 minutes | Griddle temperature: 400-450°F

Prepare Ingredients

- 8 lamb chops
- 4 cloves of garlic, minced
- 4 tbsp butter, melted
- 1 tsp chopped fresh rosemary
- 1 tsp chopped fresh thyme
- 1 tsp salt
- 1 tsp black pepper

Start the Griddle

1. Preheat the gas griddle to 400-450°F.
2. In a small bowl, mix together the garlic, butter, rosemary, thyme, salt, and pepper.
3. Brush the lamb chops with the butter mixture.
4. Place the lamb chops on the griddle and cook for 4-5 minutes on each side or until they are cooked to your desired doneness.
5. Serve the lamb chops hot.

Nutritional Value (Per Serving)

- Caloric content: 450-500 calories
- Protein: 30-35 grams & Fat: 40-45 grams
- Carbohydrates: 2-5 grams
- Fiber: 0 grams & Sugar: 0 grams
- Cholesterol: 120-140 mg
- Saturated Fat: 20-25 grams

Garlic & Rosemary Grilled Lamb Chops

The lamb chops are marinated in a flavorful garlic and rosemary mixture, which infuses the meat with a rich, herbaceous flavor.

Serving size: 4 people | Preparation time: 20 minutes

Grilling time: 8-10 minutes | Griddle temperature: 425-450°F

Prepare Ingredients

- 8 lamb chops
- 4 cloves of garlic, minced
- 2 tbsp olive oil
- 1 tsp chopped fresh rosemary
- 1 tsp salt
- 1 tsp black pepper

Start the Griddle

1. In a small bowl, mix together the garlic, olive oil, rosemary, salt, and pepper. Rub the mixture all over the lamb chops, making sure to coat them evenly. Cover the chops and refrigerate for at least 30 minutes or overnight. Preheat the gas griddle to 425-450°F. Remove the lamb chops from the marinade and shake off any excess marinade.
2. Place the lamb chops on the griddle and cook for 4-5 minutes on each side or until they are cooked to your desired doneness.
3. Serve the lamb chops hot.

Nutritional Value (Per Serving)

- Caloric content: 250-300 calories
- Protein: 25-30 grams
- Fat: 20-25 grams
- Carbohydrates: 0-2 grams
- Fiber: 0 grams
- Sugar: 0 grams

☆ ☆ ☆ ☆ ☆

Dessert Recipes

Griddle Monkey Bread With Biscuits

Desserts are what separates a master griddle chef from the layman. The dish is both sweet and flavorful, with a nice crunchy texture, and makes for a perfect way to enjoy a comforting treat with family and friends.

Serving size: 6-8 people | Preparation time: 20 minutes

Grilling time: 8-10 minutes | Griddle temperature: 375-400°F

Prepare Ingredients

- 1 can of refrigerated biscuits
- 1/2 cup granulated sugar
- 1 tsp ground cinnamon
- 1/4 cup butter, melted
- 1/4 cup brown sugar
- 1/4 cup chopped pecans

Start the Griddle

1. Cut the biscuits into quarters and place them in a large bowl.
2. In a small bowl, mix together the granulated sugar and cinnamon.
3. Add the sugar mixture to the biscuits and toss until the biscuits are evenly coated.
4. In another small bowl, mix together the melted butter, brown sugar, and chopped pecans.
5. Preheat the gas griddle to 375-400°F.
6. Place the biscuit mixture on the griddle and cook for 4-5 minutes per side or until they are golden brown.
7. Remove the biscuits from the griddle and let them rest for a few minutes.
8. Drizzle the butter mixture over the biscuits and toss to coat evenly.
9. Serve the monkey bread hot and enjoy!

Nutritional Value (Per Serving)

- Caloric content: 400-500 calories
- Protein: 4-5 grams
- Fat: 20-25 grams
- Carbohydrates: 40-50 grams
- Sugar: 20-25 grams
- Fiber: 1-2 grams

Grilled Smore's Pizza

This recipe takes advantage of the rich and flavorful combination of chocolate, marshmallow, and graham crackers, which are the traditional ingredients in s'mores.

Serving size: 8 people | Preparation time: 10 minutes

Grilling time: 8-10 minutes | Griddle temperature: 375-400°F

Prepare Ingredients
- 1 pre-made pizza crust
- 1 cup chocolate chips
- 1 cup marshmallow fluff
- 1/4 cup graham cracker crumbs

Start the Griddle
1. Preheat the gas griddle to 375-400°F. Place the pizza crust on the griddle and cook for 2-3 minutes per side or until it is lightly golden brown.
2. Remove the crust from the griddle and let it rest for a few minutes. Spread the chocolate chips and marshmallow fluff over the crust. Sprinkle the graham cracker crumbs on top of the pizza. Place the pizza back on the griddle and cook for another 2-3 minutes or until the chocolate is melted and the marshmallow is golden brown.
3. Remove the pizza from the griddle and let it rest for a few minutes. Cut the pizza into slices and serve warm.

Nutritional Value (Per Serving)
- Caloric content: 500-600 calories
- Protein: 8-10 grams
- Fat: 20-25 grams
- Carbohydrates: 60-70 grams
- Fiber: 1-2 grams
- Sugar: 30-35 grams

Griddle Cinnamon Rolls

The rolls are sweet and flavorful, with a nice gooey texture and are a delicious and easy-to-make breakfast treat that is perfect for a special occasion or a casual weekend morning.

Serving size: 8 people | Preparation time: 20 minutes

Rising time: 1 hour | Grilling time: 8-10 minutes

Griddle temperature: 375-400°F

Prepare Ingredients

- 1 package active dry yeast
- 1/4 cup warm water
- 1/4 cup granulated sugar
- 1/2 cup milk
- 1/4 cup butter
- 1 egg
- 1 tsp salt
- 3-4 cups all-purpose flour
- 1/2 cup brown sugar
- 1 tsp ground cinnamon
- 1/4 cup butter, melted
- 1/4 cup granulated sugar

Start the Griddle

1. In a small bowl, combine the yeast, warm water, and 1/4 cup of granulated sugar. Let stand for 10 minutes or until the mixture becomes frothy.
2. In a medium saucepan, heat the milk and butter until the butter is melted. Remove from heat and let cool to lukewarm.
3. In a large bowl, beat the egg and salt. Add the yeast mixture and the milk mixture. Stir in the flour, 1 cup at a time, until the dough comes together and is easy to handle.
4. Knead the dough for about 8-10 minutes or until it becomes

smooth and elastic.
5. Place the dough in a greased bowl, cover it with a towel, and let it rise in a warm place for about 1 hour or until it has doubled in size.
6. Preheat the gas griddle to 375-400°F.
7. Roll out the dough into a large rectangle.
8. In a small bowl, mix together the brown sugar and cinnamon.
9. Spread the melted butter over the dough, then sprinkle the sugar mixture on top.
10. Roll up the dough tightly and cut into 8-10 slices.
11. Place the cinnamon rolls on the griddle and cook for 4-5 minutes per side or until they are golden brown.
12. Remove the cinnamon rolls from the griddle and let them rest for a few minutes.
13. Serve the cinnamon rolls warm.

Nutritional Value (Per Serving)

- Caloric content: 400-500 calories
- Protein: 5-6 grams
- Fat: 20-25 grams
- Carbohydrates: 50-60 grams
- Fiber: 1-2 grams
- Sugar: 20-25 grams

Extra Lofty Griddle Cakes

This recipe yields pancakes that are light and fluffy, with a nice balance of sweetness and a crispy exterior. The recipe can be easily modified to suit your preferences, by using different types of flours, sweeteners, or add-ins such as blueberries, chocolate chips, or nuts.

Serving size: 8 people | Preparation time: 15 minutes

Cooking time: 8-10 minutes | Griddle temperature: 375-400°F

Prepare Ingredients

- 2 cups all-purpose flour
- 2 tsp baking powder
- 1 tsp baking soda
- 1/4 tsp salt
- 1/4 cup sugar
- 1 egg
- 1 cup milk
- 1/4 cup melted butter
- 1 tsp vanilla extract

Start the Griddle

1. In a large bowl, whisk together the flour, baking powder, baking soda, salt and sugar.
2. In a separate bowl, beat the egg, then add the milk, melted butter and vanilla extract. Mix well.
3. Add the wet ingredients to the dry ingredients and mix until just combined. Do not overmix.
4. Preheat the gas griddle to 375-400°F.
5. Use a ladle to pour the batter onto the griddle.
6. Cook the pancakes for 2-3 minutes per side or until they are golden brown and cooked through.
7. Remove the pancakes from the griddle and let them rest for a few minutes.
8. Serve the pancakes warm with butter and syrup.

Nutritional Value (Per Serving)

- Caloric content: 400-450 calories
- Protein: 8-10 grams
- Fat: 20-25 grams
- Carbohydrates: 40-50 grams
- Fiber: 1-2 grams
- Sugar: 10-15 grams

Chocolate Griddle Cakes

If there is one way to make griddle cakes a magical gastronomical experience for chocolate lovers is by adding chocolate to them. And this is how you do it.

Serving size: 8 people | Preparation time: 15 minutes

Cooking time: 8-10 minutes | Griddle temperature: 375-400°F

Prepare Ingredients

- 2 cups all-purpose flour
- 1/2 cup cocoa powder
- 1 tsp baking powder
- 1 tsp baking soda
- 1/4 tsp salt
- 1/4 cup sugar
- 1 egg
- 1 cup milk
- 1/4 cup melted butter
- 1 tsp vanilla extract
- 1/2 cup chocolate chips

Start the Griddle

1. In a large bowl, whisk together the flour, cocoa powder, baking powder, baking soda, salt, and sugar.
2. In a separate bowl, beat the egg, then add the milk, melted butter, and vanilla extract. Mix well.
3. Add the wet ingredients to the dry ingredients and mix until just combined. Stir in the chocolate chips. Do not over-mix.
4. Preheat the gas griddle to 375-400°F.
5. Use a ladle to pour the batter onto the griddle.
6. Cook the pancakes for 2-3 minutes per side or until they are golden brown and cooked through.
7. Remove the pancakes from the griddle and let them rest for a few minutes.

8. Serve the pancakes warm with butter and syrup.

Nutritional Value (Per Serving)

- Caloric content: 500-550 calories
- Protein: 8-10 grams
- Fat: 25-30 grams
- Carbohydrates: 55-65 grams
- Fiber: 2-3 grams
- Sugar: 20-25 grams

Rum-Glazed Griddled Pineapple

Rum-Glazed Griddled Pineapple is a delicious and easy-to-make dessert that yields pineapple that is sweet, juicy, and slightly caramelized, with a nice balance of flavor and a crispy exterior.

Serving size: 8 people | Preparation time: 10 minutes

Cooking time: 8-10 minutes | Griddle temperature: 375-400°F

Prepare Ingredients

- fresh pineapple, peeled and cored
- 1/4 cup dark rum
- 1/4 cup brown sugar
- 1/4 cup butter
- 1 tsp vanilla extract

Start the Griddle

1. Cut the pineapple into 1-inch thick slices.
2. In a small saucepan, combine the rum, brown sugar, butter, and vanilla extract.
3. Cook over medium heat, stirring constantly until the sugar and butter have melted and the mixture is smooth.
4. Preheat the gas griddle to 375-400°F.
5. Place the pineapple slices on the griddle and brush the top of the pineapple with the rum glaze.
6. Cook the pineapple for 4-5 minutes per side or until they are golden brown and heated through.
7. Remove the pineapple slices from the griddle and let them rest for a few minutes.
8. Serve the pineapple warm.

Nutritional Value (Per Serving)

- Caloric content: 200-250 calories
- Protein: 1-2 grams
- Fat: 10-12 grams

- Carbohydrates: 25-30 grams
- Fiber: 2-3 grams
- Sugar: 20-25 grams

www.ingramcontent.com/pod-product-compliance
Lightning Source LLC
Chambersburg PA
CBHW050301120526
44590CB00016B/2449